# SAFE WORDS

# safe words

poems

## Michelle Brown

Palimpsest Press
1171 Eastlawn Ave.
Windsor, Ontario. N8S 3J1
www.palimpsestpress.ca

Book and cover design by Kate Hargreaves (CorusKate Design)
Edited by Jim Johnstone

Palimpsest Press would like to thank the Canada Council for the Arts,
and the Ontario Arts Council for their support of our publishing
program. We also acknowledge the assistance of the Government of
Ontario through the Ontario Book Publishing Tax Credit.

*Library and Archives Canada Cataloguing in Publication*

Brown, Michelle, 1989-, author
Safe words / Michelle Brown.

Poems.
ISBN 978-1-926794-72-3 (softcover)

I. Title.

PS8603.R6923S24 2018        C811'.6        C2017-907128-9

PRINTED AND BOUND IN CANADA

*For Vincent—you're all the good parts*

# contents

safe words

Two years to write this book
is how many in dog years?

I was too shy
to play 'bi' in Scrabble.

If I had no name, could you still find me?
I'm short and have brown hair.

*She didn't read the sign*, they whispered.
The bitches. They watched me drown.

One of those was the one true thing.
Catch it if you can.

I pat my dog and weep.
Why won't he talk to me?

By the time this book is finished,
will we have grown apart?

I fell in love with my husband.
It's no longer an interesting story.

*Nothing in life is boring*, said my mother.
I just posted my first photo to Instagram in a while.

Kayla and Jessie and Vincent.
Kayla and Jessie and Vincent.

Writing it down
commits you.

When I turn 30,
I'll have two years to write another book.

Japan is there. Home is there.
Until their twin earthquakes vanish them.

I don't like to lay on your chest.
If you're living, will you die?

My first love was a letter.
My last love is a black book.

If my dog names my first born,
will I love them both equally?

It's true what they've been saying about me.
I *am* your brown-eyed girl.

A man approached holding a stick.
It was just a hockey stick.

## SIXTEEN

I had my septum pierced by a man
in a small room. Right through

the moment of upper adolescence.
Eyes closed and looking towards

the pain. Sulphur and pine and red blood moving.

      Isn't this what you wanted for me?
      To live momentarily. Out of my head

and into the mirror.
He finished the circle with a silver ball

to twirl and remove.

Stop, tear. I am the maker of what's shown on my face.
Now, and forever, happiness.

## ALTAR GIRLS

Like the lotus and the fern before,
here we go unraveling.

If the bell sounds three times,
all will be forgotten,

with a mouthful of blood
and a wink to the audience.

If he will love me forever & ever,
make his home in my heart,

for thine is whatever
flows between our white dresses,

spirit or spit or the long childhood
that comes afterwards.

That I could be laid out
unceremoniously,

without red carpet or petals,
only two hands behind me,

dug into. The book says
that all of us, with this heavy

cross to bear, can make one final
bow to our suitors before crossing

that aisle, and I'm not sure
to whom this devotion should go,

as we skip up the altar,
lacing our gowns.

## DAILY ROUTINE

A wake. A new party day.
A cup of cheer, black.
A roll over, then back.

A last night.
A hook was thread.
A tug. A rip. I thought

A lot of thoughts before birth.
Is there A or B
amount of time left?

## STREAKER

If I'd been sitting higher up in the bleachers
If I'd considered my position

If I'd imagined it before it happened
If you hadn't unzipped yourself

If it had been pink and soft like a baby
If it had been a gift to me

If the screams hadn't set you off like a deer
If the bell hadn't been ringing so loudly

If the bell hadn't rung and the shuffle home started
If you'd had more than a minute of freedom

If I'd caught up to you
If you'd pulled my socks off with your teeth

If you'd hid me in the parentless basement
If you'd hit the drum low with your shin

If the sun hadn't set so early
If you hadn't had to bundle

If I didn't have to get so much older
If I'd stayed calm with you

If we could pass on the street now
If you could pause before running

If I was your first audience
If you were my first real feeling

## ON NOT BECOMING FAMOUS

There will be unprecedented heat waves through the weekend
       and Beyoncé will be playing on the radio,

and Beyoncé will be singing Ella Fitzgerald in reverse, in sequins,
       and I will have done sixty squats and then slept,

slept through most of the talk shows, through half of the nightly news,
       awoken to a vision of myself in sequins

lifting a thigh onto a gloved hand,
       offering my throat to the spotlight. To the wonderful critics.

To the dazzling critics. To the morning news.
       To the short man in the suit telling me it will rain today,

or maybe tomorrow, telling me until I have to go outside to grocery,
       to laundry, to sex, to wade, to feed, to walk.

Tomorrow, to the dance hall! To the barre, the sharp line of nape
       to nipple, to torso, together we détente. God,

I just want the big break. The swooping arc of life to finish in sequined
       dirt. To be buried under a chorus line, kicking.

## ALL THE PARTIES I'VE EVER BEEN TO

I thought I was a drinker until I stood up.

I took the wrong shoes and then threw the wrong shoes in the bushes.

I threw up in a shoe.

I threw a big party and didn't show.

The ambulance lost power. The ambulance was like any other car.

Counting down the traffic lights.

There won't be another time like this.

That was the promise.

Dana tried to put his whole fist in Kayla's mouth.

He was weird, even then.

I took a photo with Joe and then a photo with Vincent.

They each loved a different me.

I opened a bottle against the wall.

No one told me I was dangerous.

I just kept getting away with it.

This time around I'd like to nap more.

Reborn from under the mountain of coats.

Surprising whoever's fingering in there.

## INVASIVE SPECIES
*for my grandmother*

*Milk Thistle*

Often called alien. Often called
non-native. *But never mind all that,*
to the mirror. All four feet of her a blossom.
Of all the adorations they left her
with, best was a milk candy from Franz.
From between the bars, his solitude
was unwavering. Luckily, her wrists
were dainty. Now she's across
the sea, her father buried below
her shirts and silks. Now she is a root.
*Hail Mary*, the coast called, and the ship
slowed to it. Best to remain composed
until winter. That's when wild things grow.

## Garlic Mustard

When Joan trims her wild gardenia, she clips
back my marigolds. I've seen her plotting over tea
with Birdie. The two of them are very old.
Old enough to know the better flower.
I have been holding at thirty-six and don't
intend to reveal much more. My driver's
license has been renewed for another fifty
years, though the pedals are further away.
My tendons have shortened and I can only drive
in heels. Once, I went for a rake in the garage
and came back with a hand full of man.
He came at me with a mustard smell
and a cat-scratched underbeard. My girls
were safely in their garden beds germinating,
so nothing died and nothing was born. But garlic
mustard remains in the dirt for thirty years,
which explains my headaches and why Joan
is being a bit of a hussy. She can't help it. It's in the soil.

*Broom, Daisy*

The marguerite daisy is a shrub-like perennial.
The Marguerite can cha-cha her way out of any strata scuffle.
The Marguerite is a boat woman. She sails and floats.
The marguerite daisy pairs well with grass.
The Marguerite smoked grass, only with a Cuban,
only then would she ever. The Marguerite married
four times and loved forever. The Marguerite kept a turtle
under her bed and surprised guests with it. The marguerite
daisy is a nice little addition to flower beds.
The Marguerite pulls broom until she's stained with it.
Until she cracks her hip, blind for a minute with age.
The broom dormant for months. Then advancing.
The broom sweeping the dance floor ahead
of her, as she re-enters the world without a partner.
The broom invades as Marguerite nimbles around it,
in heels, with petals like a frame around her.
The Marguerite pulls marguerite daisies for vases and giggles.
Because the Marguerite grows elsewhere, in a condo
on the coast, kicking her heels at her timeline.

*Policeman's Helmet*

Her daughter and grandson were already
dead when he arrived, hat in hand,
so why not invite him in for tea?
Uniform hung, he recorded a tape,
*off the record*, about how the dead
were dust that danced on the boombox,
threads dangling from a bust,
thirsty roots, water pooling in the basement.
Four years later, he gave her a new name:
*fleur de Lee*. He changed her desktop
picture to an MS Paint heart.
Later, he grew shingled, shuttering
like a window and leaving her with all his shirts.
His drum kit still lords over the living
room, shaking at every storm or family
dinner. The cymbals crash at the tremor
of her hand. She goes on like this,
dancing with the stars from her easy chair;
naming them as daughter, daughter,
drum, dust, daughter.

## ADVERTISING

I made a mark. I hurt the world.
Like a weeping wave,
I pored over the bucket
that I poured my thoughts into.

I wept. I waved.
I worried the path
that I poured my thoughts into
would grow like a steel tower

and I worried the path
until, at my desk,
I grew like a steel tower
and pushed through the pink

at the seat of the heart.
To where people live
in their giant pink moments.
Where a dream puffs like a meringue

that a child holds
before eating it alive.
The dream is that we live to do good.
Tumbling through downtown

as the streetcar tracks gnash at our heels.
Nothing sinking. Nothing marred.
Held above our eyes like a hand blocking sun.
All I can do is respectfully decline.

I made a mark. I hurt the world.
I filled my bucket with their sand castles.

# YOUTUBE COMMERCIAL

Two middle-aged sweaters
climb into the dryer to die.

Skip.

A makeup tutorial
where a girl kisses
her best friend to try it.

Skip.

A grassy knoll covered
with plush toys.
They're sunbathing.

Skip.

A bottle of Coors makes
a break for it.
Dogs get drunk.

Skip.

This one's just a bald guy
crying?

Skip.

This one's a bottle of Budweiser
doing a parody of the Coors one.
The hashtags are convincing.

Skip.

A woman is crying.
I am crying.
Strings abound.

Skip, obviously.

A stranger bumps into another
stranger while texting. They kiss
then sell me insurance.

Skip.

But I buy it.

A Sri Lankan dog drinks mud
out of a pothole. Gets drunk.
I buy it.

Skip.

I'll buy it.

Skip.

A woman sits at the back
of her own mind. Removes her
cardigan.

Skip.

A thought.

Skip. Skip. Skip.
Until I skip what was playing after it.

The one where the parrot
bobs to *I Want It That Way*.

Crest up. Her little joy
on display.

# AFTER PARTY<sup>™</sup>

1.

She worries over every grain of capiscum extract
and volminicum. She worries about her liver,
learns from the box how easily it can flop over

like a sad, brown dog. Her father set her up here
and her mother pushed her over. At the After Party™
Party Cure Pill factory, she works in Measuring and Packing,

figuring how long, in grains, it takes her day to flip.
When her husband calls, she flips to accept,
then flips shut. His voice is hoary and rich.

She's tired. She's *tapped out*. Once, she passed out
under a table and slept until her neighbour kneed her.
Outside, the refuse bucket wobbles with technicoloured

*moringa*, supplying key antioxidant transport to the lymphs
of teenage skinbags drunk off their own tallness.
A hangover might be just the way to quiet.

So she called in with one. Now she sits by the train,
watching a group of young men tack their maps
together and trade sips from a brown liver.

If she were to open her hand and offer a cure,
could she too be redeemed? Swaddled in white
down and fed pizza? Drowned in the river of amyla

fruit run-off, the most giving superfood
and a bitch to scrub out of concrete.
Every hope was hers.

Every grain of it. She walked on the tracks
until she couldn't keep herself straight.
The pills were burning a hole

in her pocket and in her stomach.
Hope is acidic and hungry, like bile,
like what the liver remembers from a past life.


2.


Blonde Jason threw himself
into dance in the dining
car with such gusto

the attendant had to fan herself in the washroom.
The train made only one stop that night,
and he ended up trackside with a bag of his own vomit

and a pair of someone else's shoes.
His new friend Arni yelled out the window
after him, *Love is shit!*

Jason thought nah.
Jason thought nah about a lot of things.
He cried and walked.

He cried for his mother.
He was lost within himself
like a train or like a car

that was being shipped far off from its makers.
He napped amongst the vipers in the knee-high grass.
There's no danger in the unseen.

When the train whittled past him, the sun was up
and so was he, up to it, up for whatever, for hitching
a ride through life like a burr on a backpack.

And like most hangovers, he was both
a little drunk and a little sick
off the world that had given so freely to him.

And the woman at the station,
with those three brown pills in her palm.
Would she, too, take the easy way out?

## MOLECULAR BASEBALL

They haven't won since I was in diapers,
but since I refresh cellularly every seven years,

I'm not even me at all. None of the players
remain either. Only their trophies and styrofoam.

So who hit the grand slam? Was it me, two,
babbling in the outfield? Or was it future me,

bending down through time
to distract the pitcher?

The ball hammered him out of his reverie
and he reinvented. Molecules swapping like likes

on a year-old wedding photo. My mother
once had to apologize for my shits and giggles.

She got the best version of me too late.
I remember her last change, when the whole house

shook with another woman's laughter.
Sometimes I get the glory whole.

Down to the core, mindful of the cyanide.
As future me says, I am too blessed

to be stressed. I've got working eardrums
and a body full of blood, that sways

when the ball whizzes past my forehead.
Like we're doing a dance, death and I.

*Whoops. Almost got ya.* It dips me and I oblige.
The crowd roars in anger at their imminent destruction.

Sacks and cells plotting
their next big comeback.

## MAIDEN NAME

It was handed down
to me like a sweater.
The discrepancies mended,
the tragedy patched.
My father, in a new
new suit, proclaimed
that I was, above all,
*herself.* And so I was,
perched between past
and future like a stuffed
dodo. I shook off
the sawdust. No longer
a maiden, suckling at bar
straws. My new name
is vampiric, darker,
waxing and waning
like espresso
on a wobbly coffee table.
Brown, still. I'm thinking
of doing a callback.
Wearing my old red sequins
out networking. Baring
my throat at the status
meeting. Incorporating
velvet. No hyphenation.
I'm full you. See what you think
of your little bird now,
who is half cat,
eating herself.

## APT 1 OF 4

The couple next door had a baby, and each night
        we woke to his baby ennui. Then there was a fire

and we lived with the smell of poorly roasted coffee
        and the smell of the sagging elevator

and missed the baby. One night I couldn't find you
        in sleep, remember? I woke to you screaming

into the shower. The hard water causes heart attacks,
        so take it easy with that. There was a turtle

living next door and I would watch him as he gurgled.
        *The boredom!* he said to me. He didn't know

any better, simple creature. The winter blew clouds across
        my hanging whites. *Mustier than ever,* said the wind.

*I'm trying,* as I threw my wine out the window. It fell
        on the sidewalk in the shape of wine thrown out the window.

## TIGER LEAPING GORGE, AFTER DESCENDING

That you didn't slip or disappear under the fog,
that I could still see your hands around my face, my wrist,
your eyes darting between the river and the back of my neck,
watchful. That I could still hear the rasp of your cough
when you inhaled, surprised you could walk seven
hours without laughing, without an earbud in, with only your black
mind as a partner. That you could love me, though I cried
through the waterfall, through the goats shuffling their rears at us,
through the rumble in the distance that was neither nature nor god,
just a scream, two boys shooting pellets at the sky.
That we could come down together, both momentarily alive,
that we could share it, this life that is half brown and half green.
That it was only a rock that slid down into the water ahead of us.

## CONFIRMATION BIAS

When our friends came back
from the same hike, two weeks later,

they came jovially, fatter, with copper kettles
tied to their luggage and rings on their fingers,

and I wasn't sure if they'd married,
or just played at it,

looking and moaning
over those same grey mountains.

As they flipped through their pictures, the same
shades appeared, the same wild goats

played as a comic hazard, and as they sat on our floor,
having returned our hiking boots in better condition,

I went into the bedroom and again and again
made myself hear the bottom drop out across the gorge,

thunder or the road crumbling,
and I can hear them say that *it wasn't so bad,*

*we just walked around it,* but I can still see the dog who turned
his head towards us, eyes white with fear,

the rock that jostled as I committed to it.
Did they look at each other as you looked back at me,

swearing, stumbling, two feet closer to the wall,
rounding the last mountain before the fog.

Edging towards
that decision.

dark
sides

Without the women squatting by the river
or the deer dining on her afterbirth,

would we have the china marked with gristle
or the red blooming beneath the white skirt?

## HELLO, IT'S ME

Even Adele couldn't throat the misery I felt,
deep into Incognito Mode

while my husband worked
over a complicated meal.

I remembered the matt at the back
of your neck, the musty whatever

of you, two teens having sex
for the tenth time ever, each body part

a little triumph, a hooked comma
in my future mumblings.

Knowing you live in a two-car
off the deepest lake on the Island's west side

is like knowing too much about anything:
it wallows in the shallows of my mind

until summer, when shins stir up
the muddiest thoughts of you.

If that was a stretch, you should
see how I used to bend out of your way

on my old route, up to the chicken place,
down way away from the yoga studio,

frankincense and sweat like a mouthful of you.
Now I'm grown and heavy-footed

and still, a tear. If that's all it takes
for me, a greeting belted out of a computer

speaker, then what did it take for you
to turn away from my *hello*: years out, when I bumped

into you between tacos at Hernandez's,
poking at the membrane

between past and passed over.
How easy to have replied. To have tied

my girlhood up in a dark bag, rather than strewn
it over my happy life like a bra across the back

of a chair, across a life like a hand across the back of a chair,
right through the speakers, through the bra, through my hair.

# CAVE OF ILLUSIONS

At the El Ray
I ordered a drink
I thought you would like
for myself.

Darker than I expected,
I said on entering
and the bartender
on overhearing.

I cancelled two taxis home.
Both drivers would've said:
you should've gone home
hours ago.

We only had dinner
because the pool was closed
and the park was close
and because you asked me to.

The pool was closed
but I was still wearing
my bathing suit
under my sweater.

Feels like I'm a dark cave, I said.
Meant to add *in.* That should've been
the only thing I said
all night.

Never go to a second location,
especially down a hallway.
Where the exit is long
and very visible.

At the back of the cave,
you said, there's another cave.
How long until we get out? I ask.
You put your card on the table.

## DOUBLE

Two of us came out
swinging, my nails dug
into her palms, and they
wrongly assumed
we were embracing.
The doctor was pleased.
While we were incubating
she whispered
*Don't screw this up*
as if she already knew
I'd be the violin player,
the daisy picker.
I don't see her often now
but when I do
it's in the rearview
or the corner booth,
and she looks like me,
just badder.

## 'YOU MEANT NOTHING' WAS SAID

You were a door down a hallway
that led to another hallway,
both converging in an alley
where only you knew the exit,

and if I were in the situation
again, I wouldn't enter it,
just acknowledge the complexity
of the passageway with a nod,

taking my own taxi,
asking to be driven out of town
the slowest way, windows down,
until we get to a parking lot

where screaming for hours
on your knees won't get you arrested
and that would've been it:
a little agony.

## IF NOT X THEN WHY

X and y met z at a party
and x and z left together—
but who's naming names?
Like apples to apples
our indiscretions are only
what our thought experiments
make them out to be.
When I woke him up with your name
I assumed we both thought: *dream.*
It's just that I'm still angry about it.
I'm angry about it for a friend.
So, say I called a cab,
a cab here being a patch of grass,
how many minutes left
until it drops me at home?
I didn't find the answer on the
back page of the rule book,
so we just lay there as the apples
fell far from the tree,
that place between A and B
where you'd lose me.

## TAKE ME ANYWHERE OR ACTUALLY
## YOU KNOW WHAT JUST TAKE ME HOME

I'm only a tourist here.

Pressing the wound.
Listening to the odd sad song.

## ITALIAN VACATION

The trees bow with dead lemons.
Chickens crash in the bushes.
My dreams are full of them.
An earthquake shook the sphere
and seawater still leaks from the sky.
A red stalk waves for me.
Each mouthful of wine a wedding.
I grab my own neck in the mirror.
I grab my own hand and squeeze.
I am far away from harm here.
I am eating well.
My skin is plump.
When darkness comes,
let it sit with me.
I can stay in this hammock.
I can behave as I should.
Geckos crawl into my shadow,
where the heavier tomatoes fall.
Wasps swarm around me.
I wonder which limb
they'll remove first.

## ONCE MORE AROUND THE BLOCK

We worked it out.
The knot.

The driver looks back and says
*life is very confusing.*

He didn't ask where I was going
or you, as our two taxis drove the same way

for a while, then yours left.
But he took me along the same old route.

I passed it all without blinking.
I'd like to remember how to get back here

in case of emergency. It's like I'm reading
from a children's book: there was a park,

there was a pool, there was a restaurant.
There was a woman and man on the corner.

One was crying.
He drops me off.

I'm not sure I'm ready to leave,
so he keeps driving.

He ends the trip at someone else's life,
and I sit there in the entrance way.

Waiting for you to come home.
Find me if you get lost.

home
alone

I collect the kites from the lawn.
Bring in the dogs from the street.
Wipe the red from the white.
Do the homework left on the table.
Make a dinner for four.

Drag the kites around the house.
Lay my head on the dog's back.
Jam on cream cheese is a lighter dessert.
Research *how*.
Season the cast iron for 480 hours.

That wing
I found in my dog's mouth,
jam on white,
does it now
belong to me?

## COMPANY PICNIC

Don and his children, Mary and her children, Alison alone.
My business slacks cut to make shorts, still impossibly

hot and natural out, another speech, *what makes a business
makes a family,* forgot to pick up maca for my wife's libido,

forgot to scoop the mould out of my work mug. There's a storm
a brewin'. Had another earthquake drill today, the four of us

squatting and laughing under the cardboard roof. Alison doing her best
Marvin Gaye. Can't stop thinking about the drip.

The coffee machine newly intelligent and sad. My wife fixes my shorts
with her purse scissors. *Later*, she says, her mouth perfumed in my ear.

She reminds me of a child, with her mouth in the berries.
*A family indeed!* says the temp. Where are my children, then?

Alison, in dreams, is curled like a bug around my pinkie.
Quaint thoughts. Got a whiff of my own skin. Reminds me

of something I let go. Climbing up the tree, I forget who I work for,
my heart an impish boyfriend. From these heights, I see my wife

at the picnic table. Her beautiful future. Her careful planning.
They're pairing up for the two-legged race. My money's on the man

who knew what was coming,
brought his best running shoes.

## EBB

My daughter standing in the water.
A knot inside me tethers. My daughter
to her knees in water. Once, I was
her carrier. Her larger thing. She didn't
listen to my tone. She didn't listen to the sea,
that pause that pools below her knees,
didn't hear it warn that it will take her
far away from me. In believing she was,
she bought the conceit. That something grand
was taking place. That her life would be hung
from a tree to dry. That her heart
would out-beat all other machines.
Small burps of gratitude as I held her to feed.
My daughter in the sea. Her simple knees.
Her two feet that tread and do these things
to me. I know defeat. That rising line.
My daughter in the sea, to her knees,
taken far away from me.

## FATHER, ON A CAMPING TRIP, REFUSES TO LEAVE HIS TENT

Not even to prolong his daughter's legacy, not for her cheeks,
red and natural on the nature walk, not for the deer
who paws the tarp as a cat might, not for any animal
who would willingly give its throat, not for his son
who wrings tears into soup before passing it through the zipper.
All night on the battle-gravel, his family treats his rage with gifts.
A night in the marital sleeping bag. His name in dirt, misspelled.
His daughter, her cheeks now concave and annoyed.
He, no longer #1, would refuse to drink from that mug.
These three mocking strangers who, no longer finding notes
in their lunchboxes, have forgotten his name entirely.
Changed theirs to resemble something worldly.
Extrafamilial. Orbital. A gift tag tied to his balls with a string.
His wife wails through the canvas. Skin tough and jumping
as if she were a walnut, or a burning tree, or gristle.
*If you must take her give me seven women in return.*
*Give them to me in order of preference. Name them youth,*
*pliancy, flexibility, smoothness, beauty, beauty, and beauty.*

# RESTAURANT REVIEW

Up from the family table, your wife who dresses evenly
but remains pear-shaped, your father in the basement, crying
into the arm of the futon you thought would comfort him,
*comfort*, even the word smells vintage, rotting floor tiles,
the smell of him rising into the dining room where your children
are less smart and more toxic than you'd hoped,
when you'd hoped for pink and blue cotton swabs,
gurgling sound effect machines.

You leave the humble meal, part frozen,
part fresh, as if your wife just grew sad mid-potato,
the desire to leave the table, go to a new easiness,
daisy-fresh tang of a neck, vintage jumper,
steak that fills the sickness in your stomach,
a flesh that is rare and warm, not loose and your own,
waiting in the basement, watching the children's cartoons,
waiting to remind you about your wife in the kitchen,
her stomach gently swaying as she bends and lifts, picks up and puts away.

## BOY, ON THE NONEXISTENCE OF THE TRICERATOPS

No trilobites, no ammonites, no longer
will I pray to a brontosaurus instead
of the Christian god. I will not admit
it's because he was taller. No titanosaur,
nor will I believe in the asteroid, the exile
where the vocal and spry were saved, no
I will not identify with the feathered anchiornis
for his supposed sensitivity, no bones will be thrown
to the circling pterodactyls. I am not one
in the lineage of the extinct. Nothing came
before me. I have no father, though I am my father's
only son. My goldfish will die without pellets,
but I will not die. I do not belong to the scaled
and floating few. No longer will I stand in the museum,
in the cavity of the tyrant, the terrible one,
and be his heart. I will not be judged for his kills
by cloaked man or meteorite. I will not die
for what is now mountainside. I will no longer
stand complicit behind my mother in fall,
beside the fallen apples, when she says *it is too bad
about the apples.* I will no longer feel bad.
I will not be remembered as I am, in the garden
with the dog's bones, weeping, categorizing.

## BETTY

My name is Betty. May I take your coat? My husband was a logger, too.
My husband was a fisherman. I have a funny story

about being tangled in his net. I can't remember it just yet, but wait
until you try my banana loaf. It's divine. My name is Betty.

My children are asleep. My children are at school. Have you noticed
that the aisles of all the stores look the same? Hard to find

what you're looking for. My name's                                      .
It's hard to remember when you all look the same.

My husband's at work. My husband worked hard
until the day he slipped. No, he's still alive. He slipped up.

You all look so refined. My name is Betty. I'm still alive.
I'm still divine. My eyes widened. When I saw it.

Saw the sunrise, of course. The sun sets differently on each coast.
I've always wanted to travel north. My husband works in finery.

My children are ages one and three, they'd love to be here
to watch me succeed. At what? At this.

They placed me here because they want me to succeed.
My children and me, we were only three

when we saw the tearing at all sides. I wanted to lie, but that dress
looks divine, the purple flowers bring out your eyes.

Yes, I do dabble in art. My name is Betty.
Please sit back down. I've made a fresh tart.

## BETSY

We're interested in buying a house. We're interested in buying a home,
I said, to hide things in. A family matter, nothing else.

Do you have anything with a terrace? With a windowsill? I have basil.
I have a son who loves this town. It's better that there are no

other kids around. We all spill things occasionally. I want a house
with locking doors. I want a home with nothing else,

just a hearth for warmth. No five-year plan. I can't see past
the lemonade stand, the after-school funk.

My husband comes home and lays face-down in bed.
The repairman came, said *there's nothing wrong.*

It is so hard to tell who is doing their job. I'm still here,
someone else is gone. In ten years I'd like to be weeding the lawn,

pulling up dandelions to steep in water. Those maligned daughters.
I'm forever indebted. I've been told that lab rats become

attached to their injectors, as they believe they're preserved out of mercy.
It's just something I heard. I prayed to a god who did what he could.

Who pulled me out tantrically, frantically. I won't be taking this today.
My husband will think it's too close to the water. Our previous houses

have always had leaks. The cupboards prone to terrible thuds.
I shouldn't say that I haven't had luck.

# MEMOIR ATTEMPTS

I can still form myself: pull up my knees, tighten my waist.

I know all the planets, their order, what they do to me

when I'm feeling. I can dress myself well. I have pardons left.

I can still be a nuisance, hoist myself onto the roof,

stomp out the raccoons. I can live with my uselessness.

I understand that the new kettle shuts off automatically.

I can parent these machines. No longer Mother Earth

in the learning garden, pulling up crooked carrots.

I know what a wall is. I can grow my children that way.

I am the note-keeper of my own destiny. I can, and do,

write a horoscope column in my notebook,

predicting that *you will die, I don't know when* to all.

I can sleep both at your feet and at your head.

I can still climb on. I can feel my parts

in their gelatinous casings. I can now afford to change

my name. There is still time to grow up to be my daughter.

I suffered with the dog who barked madly through his death.

I thought if I wrote my life, I would be permitted to leave it.

having
done my
penance
let's try
this again

You lost your body.
You grew a husk.

You figured it out.
Breast small and mighty.

Take your time.
Do the renaming.

Grow green again.
Or a deeper colour.

I bring you along.
I press your bruise.

I left space for you
to redecorate.

Isn't it amazing to no longer
be left in the rain?

## DOG FARM

They're sent here
to the open field, defamilied,
when they get too familiar.

They run like wild grass
stuck to a shoe.
Begging to sit.

If you held out your hand,
would they reach you?
Would you tell them no?

Could you please?
If every night
is someone's big night,

the world can't sustain
that many single tears
running down

that many seatbelts.
I was sent here
to be solitary, a monk

escaping to the hill
to see the sun bludgeoning in.
To feel violent again.

No dog is unwanted,
I reassure myself
as they circle me.

No, they say.
But these aren't our names.
And where are our leashes?

## TWENTY-SEVEN

It wasn't anything deeper.
Just a single bug along
the lake's surface that startled me
enough to fasten my bra,
feel my way back up the stairs to you.

# WHEN YOU GO OUT IN THE WORLD TODAY

Be sure of a big surprise. Mind your gaps,
check your chairs for tacks. Scrub yourself

of identifiable marks, so I can say
*not mine* when they bring your effects.

Don't be a martyr, a lightning rod.
Drive away from the direction of fog.

Quietly disagree with the neighbour's bass.
Leave me notes that say *you're still okay*.

Teach me the hardest parts of your poems.
Record my name on tape.

Look both ways. Check your headaches.
Leave the reddest meat to a ruddier man.

Open every can. Kiss both breasts.
Pre-attend our children's pirouettes.

Give the stranger your wallet. Smoke only meat.
Be like your grandfather. Ninety-three.

## ENERGIZER

Everyone is born to die, though some do it
under a porch light looking at the forest line,
and others from the defibrillator.
Is it wrong to want from my batteries
what I want from life? To just work.
In fact, there is no one word for 'life sick',
making it harder to remember that after the night
of smashed concords and stewed bones
comes the tunnel of light, far away still,
moving from periphery to focus, then fading
for twenty years, more if you're lucky.
Until you've wound yourself up in a corner
like a mechanical dog. Spending your energy.

## VOWS

What I'm about to claim is neither true
nor false, a grey answer when the choices

were red and purple, but I don't remember
stepping into that October water with you,

or what the key unlocked that we let slip,
laughing, only to see it wash up years later,

after we'd left that door unworried about. I don't
even remember the question, if it had been asked,

but there was your body, supported by reflection,
asking anyways. There I said yes.

Not below any lights or cameras or action.
And I didn't speak again, even as the world asked,

the heat asked, the dirt from your thumb
asked, until now, when I am asking you to look back

at the shaded mountain and tell me that it was so
beautiful that you couldn't then, but are asking me now.

## IN THE KITCHEN

Here is where I settled
into what might be my life.

I used to let the apples wine.
We wore ourselves well,

only small holes around the armpits
and collar. I let the wine win

mostly. I was mad about you.
I'll omit the parts

where you breathed in and out
at the kitchen table.

Or when you left me at the ferry
with just a doughnut to my name.

A sadness too simple,
in hindsight.

Now let me soak in the pans
alight and rowed,

the fruits, in their intended
skins, cored

and stewed with sugar—
the part of you I'll never get to.

I love you and I'll never
know you.

But *that is my husband* I say,
giddy at all the parts of you that circle me

like sweet ghosts, bringing me
dinner, every night, at the old table.

## ESCAPE FROM THE DOG FARM

I was told I was being sent to live with friends.
That there would be parties to run with.
That I would be afforded adequate stimulation.

I can't be blamed for testing the fence.
Just close enough to his hand I could call it a brush.
I'm still an approximation of good.

I'm still what many consider a healthy woman running.
From the road, my escape route looks like a jog.
Something taken at regular intervals.

Inside each life is another, like a doll.
My part of the deal was that my love
would be endless, like a tap stuck open.

When you look at it whole, a discography played
while you sleep, the crumbs have already been swept.
We are healthy. Our muscles toned. Our eyes white.

But someone is digging a hole out.

## STORIES

HEY Jessie yelled from the 19th floor.
Kayla was already up there, with striped tights
and sweet hair. Vincent was puffing alongside
me, young as a pup. I wasn't born yet.

But in the night, the ultrasound
showed signs of growth. As I lay under the table,
counting gum, I started to roll my shoulders back.
It could've been the moon like a horse's eye.

I thought I had power in my hands. Kayla joined to me
for a while and never left. Jessie pulled us
under the arms to the balcony
where we yelled HEY at some more people.

I thought she was sad when I met her.
Now we're 27 and 29 stories up, respectively.
I thought we were sad
until I thought of something else.

That first night, I ran down all those stairs,
19 flights, back down to infancy. I slumped towards the end.
Slept against a planter. And Jessie and Kayla
and Vincent woke me up like

HEY. HEY. MICHELLE.
WE THOUGHT WE'D NEVER FIND YOU.

# acknowledgements

Thank you to *Arc Poetry Magazine*, *Contemporary Verse 2*, *The Malahat Review*, *Minola Review*, *PRISM International*, *The Puritan*, and *The Walrus* for publishing these poems in their former shapes.

Some poems also appeared previously in the following chapbooks: *Foreign Experts Building* (Desert Pets Press) *365 Days* (Desert Pets Press) and *Toronto Series* (Frog Hollow Press).

Infinite love, awe and appreciation for Mom, Dad, Andrea & Ms. Marguerite Lee—my gratitude is woven through each word.

Kayla and Jessie, thank you for finding me!

To my early mentors Ross Demmings, Linda DiFelice, Steven Price, Carla Funk, Lorna Crozier and Tim Lilburn—for your generosity and dogged belief in me.

Jim Johnstone, thank you for taking a chance on this book and for making it so much better. It has been a real joy working with you. To Aimee Parent Dunn and everyone at Palimpsest Press, for your unrelenting support. And to Kate Hargreaves, for reading my mind and designing the cover of my (actual) dreams.

Bardia, Jess, Phoebe, Catriona, Laura, Daniel, Ted—for fixing my tenses & tendencies, for being such great first readers.

To the Ontario Arts Council, for supporting this book and the work of so many others.

To my best dog Bo—you have permission to chew one copy!

And to my husband and partner in all, Vincent—you've made this life the best adventure.

Originally from Victoria, BC, **MICHELLE BROWN** lives in Toronto with her husband and three-legged dog Bo. *Safe Words* is her first full-length collection.